Word in a Minute

Steps for Performing Basic Tasks in Microsoft Office 2010

Diane L. Martin
My PC Associate NYC

First Edition

Word in a Minute

Steps for Performing Basic Tasks in Microsoft Office 2010

Diane L. Martin

My PC Associate NYC

DISCLAIMER

Acknowledgements

The author gratefully acknowledges the support and encouragement of Latoya Trowers Bell, Judy Ganeles Wilson, Sharon Cunningham, Anahu Guzman, Francine Martin, and Rajasekhar Vangapaty.

Dedication

To my niece Justine,

Anything is possible, if you believe.

Collect the Entire

Office in a Minute Series

  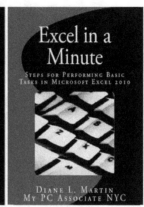

This comprehensive edition includes
Word, Excel, OneNote and PowerPoint.

Available online

mypcassociate.com
Amazon.com
barnesandnoble.com

My PC Associate NYC

Compute, Excel and Advance!

Table of Contents

Short Table of Contents

About this Book

The purpose of this Book is to serve as a quick tutorial for purchasers of Microsoft Word 2010 who are relatively unfamiliar with the application's features, functions and benefits.   If you want to learn the most salient features of this very robust application, you have come to the right place. Through this handy tutorial, you will learn how to:

- Open an existing file
- Create a new document
- Save a document
- Print a document
- Change print options
- Use the spelling and grammar feature
- Apply character formatting using bold, underline or italics
- Apply page layout controls
- Format paragraphs using the left, center right, and justify alignment buttons
- Use the bullets and numbering feature.
- Insert a picture into a document
- Place shapes into a document
- Access and manipulate templates
- Use the SmartArt feature
- Insert a header or footer into a document
- Insert a table into a document

The wonderful thing about Word is that most features and functions are capable of being performed in one minute or less. Practice using them on a regular basis, and before you know it, you will begin to recall them effortlessly.

Happy Computing!

"Let us watch well our beginnings and results will manage themselves."

Alexander Clark

CHAPTER 1
GETTING STARTED

- ***Launch Microsoft Word***
- ***Identify Screen Elements***
- ***Select and Edit Text***
- ***Save a Document***
- ***Close an Existing Document***
- ***Open an Existing Document***
- ***Create a New Document***

🕐 *The Estimated Time to Complete These Tasks is 15 minutes.*

Launching the Microsoft Word Application

Open the Microsoft Word application installed on your computer by clicking on the Office Start button. You will find this button located in the lower left-hand corner of your desktop. Locate the Microsoft Word icon and then double-click your mouse button; this will launch the application.

The Microsoft Word Environment

Figure 1

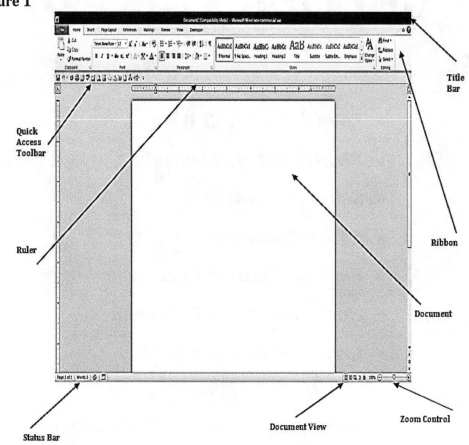

Take a few minutes to become familiar with the screen elements depicted in Figure 1. The Microsoft Word application opens with nine tabs respectively named File, Home, Insert, Page Layout, References, Mailings, Review, View and Developer. Each tab has a ribbon organized into groups. For example, look at the Home tab, and notice the buttons within the Font group. This group contains buttons related to changing the appearance of text, and allows you to apply bold, underline or italics to basic text.

Selecting and Editing Text

After Microsoft Word opens to a brand new document, you may simply begin typing; however, if you hope to become proficient, you should understand a little more about the fundamentals of text editing in Microsoft Word.

Observe that as you type, a cursor (|) like this one shifts to the right with each keystroke. Move your mouse around a bit, and you will likely see this (|). This is your insertion pointer.

Figure 2

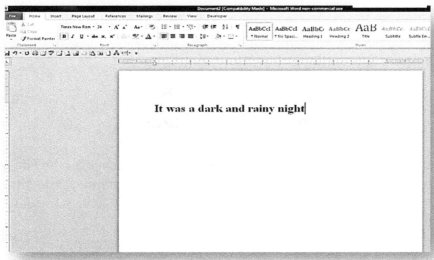

The act of merely typing your text is straightforward; however, when it comes to editing what you have typed, managing your cursor and insertion beam will be invaluable. For example, suppose you want to edit the text depicted in Figure 2.

Start by typing the words "It was a dark and rainy night." If you decide to change the word rainy to stormy, you have several options. You can place your cursor at the end of the line and hit the backspace key 11 times to delete all of the characters up to the word "and", or you can click your mouse anywhere within the word rainy and double-click your left mouse button. When you double-click on the word **rainy,** it becomes highlighted. Now type the word stormy. Whenever you want to change or edit text in Word, you must first select that text by moving your mouse over the text and then double-clicking your left mouse button.

Selecting Text

1. Hover with your mouse over the desired text.

2. Double-click your left mouse button.

3. Locate and press the delete key on your keyboard or type alternative text.

Saving a Document

1. Click on the File tab.

2. Select the Save menu option.

3. Type a name for your document.

4. Click on the Save button.

Close an Existing Document

When you are finished working on your document, simply click on the File tab and then choose the Close icon located near the top of the menu. If you have not already saved your file, you will be prompted to do so. Click on the Save button if you want to save your changes.

Figure 3

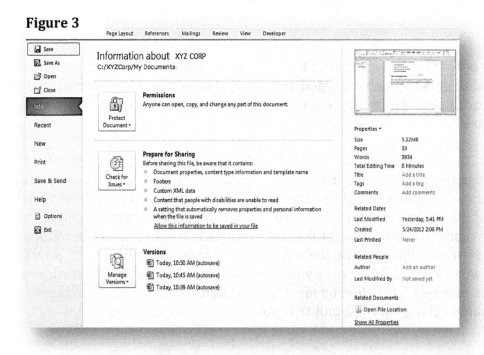

Opening an Existing Document

An existing document is one that has previously been saved to your hard disk, flash drive or floppy drive. You can click on the File tab to access Word's Backstage View, and then you can select the Open button. Alternatively, you can select the Recent menu option to view a list of recently opened files. See Figure 4 below.

To Open an Existing Document

1. Click on the File tab.

2. Click on the Open or Recent menu option.

3. Select the desired file.

4. Click on the Open button.

Figure 4

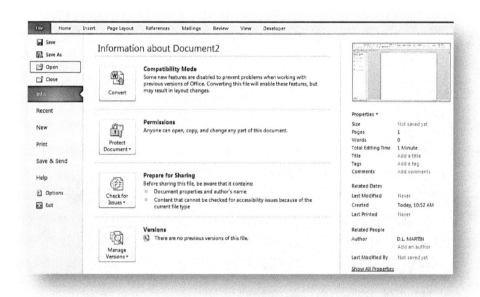

Other useful options on the File tab include Save and Send. This feature will allow you to both save and e-mail a copy of your document. The document can be sent as an attachment or can be printed within the e-mail message form.

As you become more comfortable with Word, try exploring the Options menu. Through the Options menu, you can customize the Word environment. See Chapter 3 for more information.

Creating a New Document

Select the File tab to initiate the opening of a new document. From the Backstage View you are provided with a variety of new document options. Word also comes with a variety of templates designed to help you quickly prepare the most common types of documents. See Chapter 4 to learn more about Microsoft Word templates.

To Create a New Document

1. Select the File tab.
2. Click on the New menu option.
3. Select the Blank document icon.
4. Click on the Create button

Figure 5

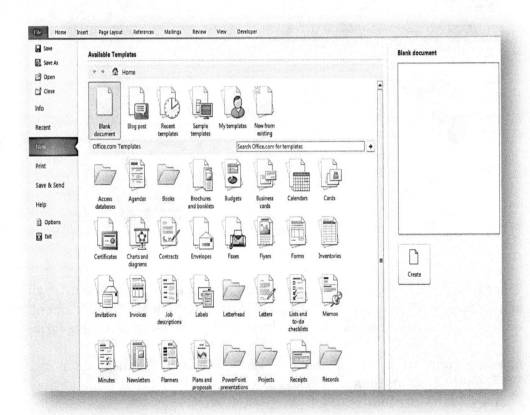

My Notes:

My Notes:

FORMATTING
A
DOCUMENT
CHAPTER 2

- ***Apply Character Formatting***

- ***Apply a New Font***

- ***Use the Format Painter***

- ***Align Text***

- ***Use Bullets & Numbering***

- ***Apply Styles***

- ***Clear Character Formatting***

- ***Undo the Last Command***

- ***Insert a Header or Footer***

- ***Use Page Layout Features***

⏱The Estimated Time to Complete These Tasks is 12 Minutes.

Applying Character Formatting

Focus your reader's attention by applying Microsoft Word's character formatting features. With one button and in about two to three seconds, you can apply **bold**, <u>underline</u>, *italicize*, **color** or change the typeface of the selected text.

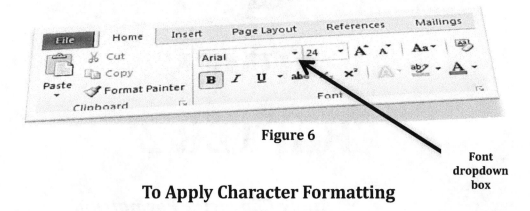

Figure 6

Font
dropdown
box

To Apply Character Formatting

1. Click on the Home tab.

2. Click into the desired text and then double-click your to select the text.

3. Click on the Bold, Italics or Underline button.

You can change the appearance of text by experimenting with various types of fonts. Word makes this very fast and easy to accomplish. Furthermore, the Word application comes with more than two-dozen serif and sans serif fonts. A serif font or typeface has little edges or feet (serifs) on each letter. Notice the letters in this paragraph. Contrast them with the word "**Paragraph**". We applied the **Arial** font to the word. Arial is an example of a sans serif. The letters have no edges or feet, in fact, the word sans means "without. " Generally, serifs are easier on the eye. Many books are written with a serif typeface; however, the font you choose will largely depend on your taste and needs. Remember one of the most efficient ways to edit text, is to first select or highlight that text, and then apply formatting options. Here is the quickest method for applying a new font to your text.

To Apply a New Font

1. Select the text to be formatted.

2. Click on the Home tab.

3. Click on the Font dropdown box and choose the desired font.

4. Click on the Font Size button to change the size of the text.

Save Time with Format Painter

Word's Format Painter feature can be a real time-saver. Imagine that you have applied bold and italics formatting to one paragraph, and wish to apply both formats to another part of your document or another word in your document. Format Painter allows you to copy the character formatting of a single word and then apply it to another word, sentence or paragraph.

To Use Format Painter

1. Click on the word that contains the desired formatting.

2. Click on the Format Painter to copy the formatting.

3. Select the desired text to apply the formatting.

Text Alignment and the Tab Key

The Microsoft Word program makes four basic text alignment options available: left, centered, right, or justified. See the Paragraph group on the Home tab in Figure 7. As an example, to center text on the page, you will want to perform these two simple steps.

1. Select the text to be centered.

2. Click on the Center Button or press (Ctrl + E).

Note: Try pressing the **Tab** key to align text every 0.5 inches along the ruler. The Tab key is great for creating tabular columns.

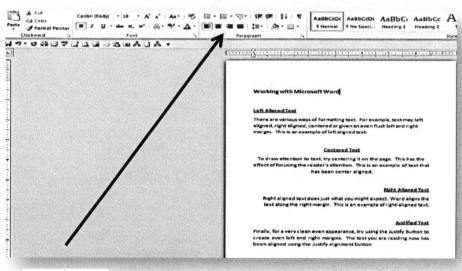

Figure 7

Formatting Text with Bullets and Numbering

Within the Paragraph group, which is located on the Home tab, you will find two extremely useful tools for formatting text. You can quickly enhance any list of items with bullets and numbering feature. Furthermore, like many features in Word, there are multiple ways to apply the bullets or numbering style to your text. Below is just one method.

To Format Text with Bullets

1. Click on the bullet button and begin typing the first item, and then press enter.

2. Type the next item, and repeat as many times as necessary.

Figure 8

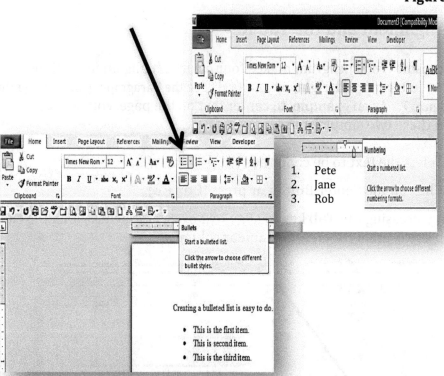

To view the variety of bullet styles that come with Microsoft Word, simply click on the Bullets dropdown box. See Figure 8 above.

Repeat the same process above to apply the numbering style. Notice too that the Numbering button also has a dropdown box with a wide selection of numbering styles.

Apply Styles to Basic Text and Save Time

Microsoft Word is chock-full of timesaving features. For example, so far you have learned how to apply character formatting to your text. However, Word's built in Styles feature takes formatting even further, by providing you with preformatted headings, titles and subtitles. See below. In addition, Word allows you to create and save your own custom formatting for use not just in your current document but in other documents as well. Think of styles as preformatting. Examine the Styles Group located on the Home tab.

Figure 9

Heading 1 is made up of the Arial Font is **bold** and has a 17-point font size. You can change the appearance of a title, subtitle or heading by selecting the text and then selecting one of the available Heading styles. Using Styles can save you the steps it normally takes to select a font, a character format and a font size.

To Apply a Heading Style

1. Click on the Home tab.
2. Select the desired text.
3. Click on the desired heading style.

To Clear Character Formatting

If you change your mind, simply click on the clear formatting button.
This will erase any formatting such as bold or underline from the selected text.

The Undo Command

Note, that you can also undo your last keystrokes by clicking the Undo button. You will find this button located on the Quick Access toolbar. Use it once and you will be hooked.

My Notes:

Inserting a Header

A header contains text that is repeated on the top of each successive page within a document. To place headers within your document perform the following steps:

1. Click on the Insert tab.

2. Click on the Header button.

3. Choose the desired header style.

4. Type the text you wish to appear on each page.

5. Click on the Close Header & Footer button.

Figure 10

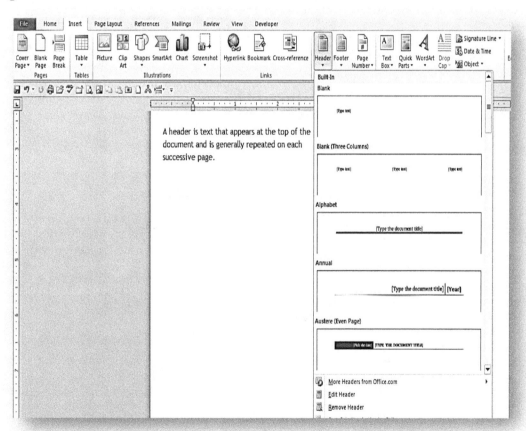

Note: When the Headers dropdown box is opened, a Headers & Footers Tools tab appears. See Figure 10 above. If you do not want the header to appear on the first page of your document, select the Different First Page button.

Inserting a Footer

A footer contains text, which is repeated on the bottom of each successive page. To place footer within your document, follow these five simple steps.

1. Click on the Insert tab.

2. Click on the Footer button.

3. Choose the desired footer style.

4. Type the text you wish to appear at the bottom of each page.

5. Click on the Close Header & Footer button.

Figure 11

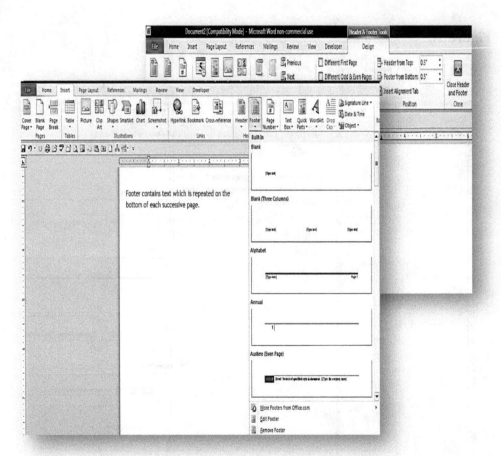

Notice that when the Footers dropdown box is opened, a Headers & Footers Tools tab appears. See Figure 11 above. If you do not want the footer to appear on the first page of your document, select the Different First Page button.

Working with the Page Layout Feature

Word makes it possible for you to control the layout of your document. If you want to change the orientation of your document from portrait to landscape, or you want to change your margin settings, you will want to become acquainted with Word's Page Layout tab. Think of the Page Layout tab as a kind of Mission Control, where there is a variety of page management tools available in one dialog box. See Figure 12 below.

To Change Margin Settings

1. Select the Page Layout tab.

2. Click on the Page Setup dropdown box.

3. Type the margin settings into the Top, Bottom, Left or Right fields as desired.

4. Click on the OK button to save your settings.

Figure 12

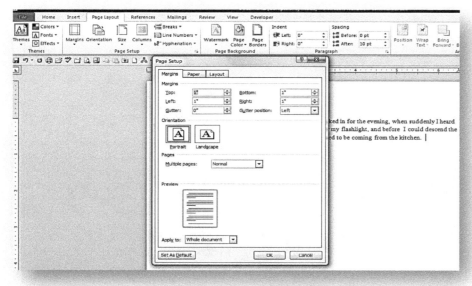

If you choose the Set As Default button, Word will apply your margin settings to all newly created documents. This same rule will apply to page orientation. Although we will not discuss it in detail here, you should know that Word gives you the option of applying settings to the whole document, or from the location of your cursor forward.

My Notes:

CHAPTER 3
SHORTCUTS &
UTILITIES

- *Use Shortcut Keys*

- *Use Cut, Copy and Paste Buttons*

- *Check Spelling & Grammar*

- *Print a Document*

- *Customize the Quick Access Menu*

- *Use the Mail Merge Feature*

🕐   *The Estimated Time to Complete These Tasks is 25 Minutes exclusive of Mail Merge.*

Using the Cut, Copy and Paste Feature

Often you will want to copy text from one location in your text to another. Alternatively, you can permanently move text to another part of your document. Word has a Cut, Copy and Paste feature that allows you to do this in mere seconds. The copied text is moved to the Clipboard. Think of the Clipboard as that magical place where data temporarily waits until you decide where to place it. There is more than one-way to copy and/or move text in Word. For example, if you want to copy text do the following:

1. Click on the Home tab.

2. Select the text you want to copy.

3. Click on the Copy button.

4. Place your mouse where you want the copied text to appear.

5. Right click your mouse button and then choose Paste.

To Remove or Cut Text

1. Select the text you want to cut.

2. Click on the Cut (scissors icon).

Short -Cut Keys

If you find yourself sitting in a cramped seat on a plane, train or an automobile, without enough space for an external mouse, try using these short-cut keystrokes. Whatever you copy is moved temporarily to Word's Clipboard. Just select the data, choose copy, and then place your cursor where you want to paste it. Press Ctrl + V and it is done!

• Copy	Ctrl + C
• Paste	Ctrl + V
• Cut	Ctrl + X

The Spelling & Grammar Feature

Microsoft Word contains a spelling and grammar-checking feature that will automatically check your document for common spelling errors. In addition, you can quickly spell check a word by selecting it, then clicking on the Spell Check button. Be advised that proper nouns and words typed in all capitals are generally **not** reviewed.

1. Click on Word's Review tab.

2. Click on the Spelling & Grammar button.

3. To accept a suggested correction, click the Change button.

Note, that Word also contains a handy thesaurus. To use the thesaurus, simply select the desired word then right click your mouse button, and choose **S**ynonyms.

- **Ignore Once**: Prompts Word to skip a word not in its dictionary -

- **Ignore All**: Prompts Word to ignore all occurrences of a word not in its dictionary

- **AutoCorrect:** Prompts Word to check its Autocorrect entries for the correct spelling of a word.

- **Options**: Opens the Proofing dialog box within the Options menu and allows you to modify spelling and grammar settings.

Printing a Document

There are several ways to initiate the printing of a Microsoft Word document. As you become more comfortable with Word, you can experiment with various methods. However, if you are new to the application, we recommend that you initiate printing from the File tab. See Figure 13, and examine the Print menu dialog box.

To Print a Document

1. Select the File tab.

2. Click on the Print Menu option to open the Printer dialog box.

3. To print the entire document, click on the Print button

4. To print selected pages, click on the settings button and enter the print range, i.e. 1-5

Figure 13

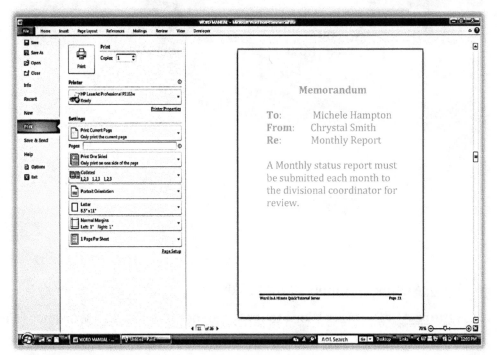

In addition to printing your document to a printer, you can also print to OneNote. OneNote is a Microsoft application that comes with MS-Office. Think of OneNote as an electronic notebook. If you do not have an immediate need for a hardcopy, OneNote may be a good place to store a digital copy of your document.

Customizing the Quick Access Toolbar and the Ribbon
MS-Word Options Menu

Place commands where you can quickly access them by customizing your Quick Access Toolbar. You can find the Quick Access toolbar just below the ribbons on each Microsoft Word tab. See Figure 14.

To Customize the Quick Access Toolbar

1. Select the File Menu.

2. Click on Options.

3. Choose Quick Access Toolbar.

4. Choose the desired command from Popular

5. Click on the Add>> button.

6. Choose the OK button.

Figure 14

Figure 15

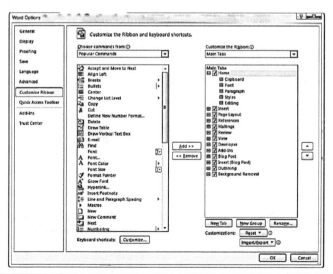

Customize the Ribbon

You can customize the Word Ribbon through the options menu. There you can choose to add or delete commands. For example, if you have a need for the E-mail command, simply click on it as depicted in Figure 15, and then click on the Add >> button.

Changing General Settings -- Options Dialog Box

Microsoft Word comes with certain default settings. For example, when you first began typing in your document, you may recall that the font was not something you initially chose. A default font is selected for you so you can begin typing as soon as you open the application. However, for a variety of reasons, you may prefer or actually require a different typeface. For this reason, you have the option of changing many of the default settings applicable to Word. To modify default settings, you will once again be required to access the Options dialog box. See Figure 16.

Click on the File tab and choose Options. There are several tabs within this dialog box, and here we will begin a brief review of the types of changes you can make to the Microsoft Word environment.

Figure 16

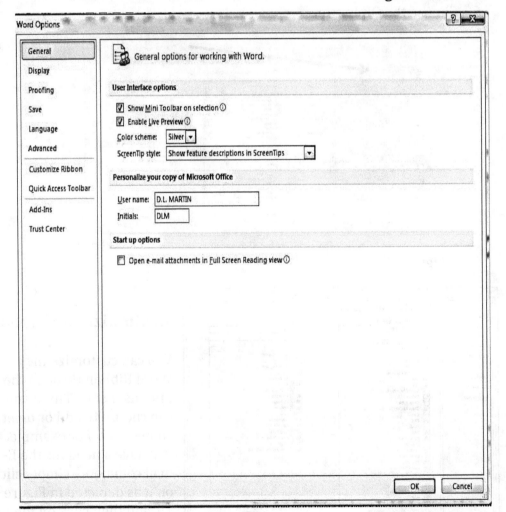

Display Options

Default display, formatting marks and printing options may be modified by selecting Display from the Word Options menu. I recommend you keep the default display and print settings until you become more proficient   in Word. When you become more familiar with Word's Page Layout and Show/Hide features, these options will become more meaningful and useful.

Figure 17

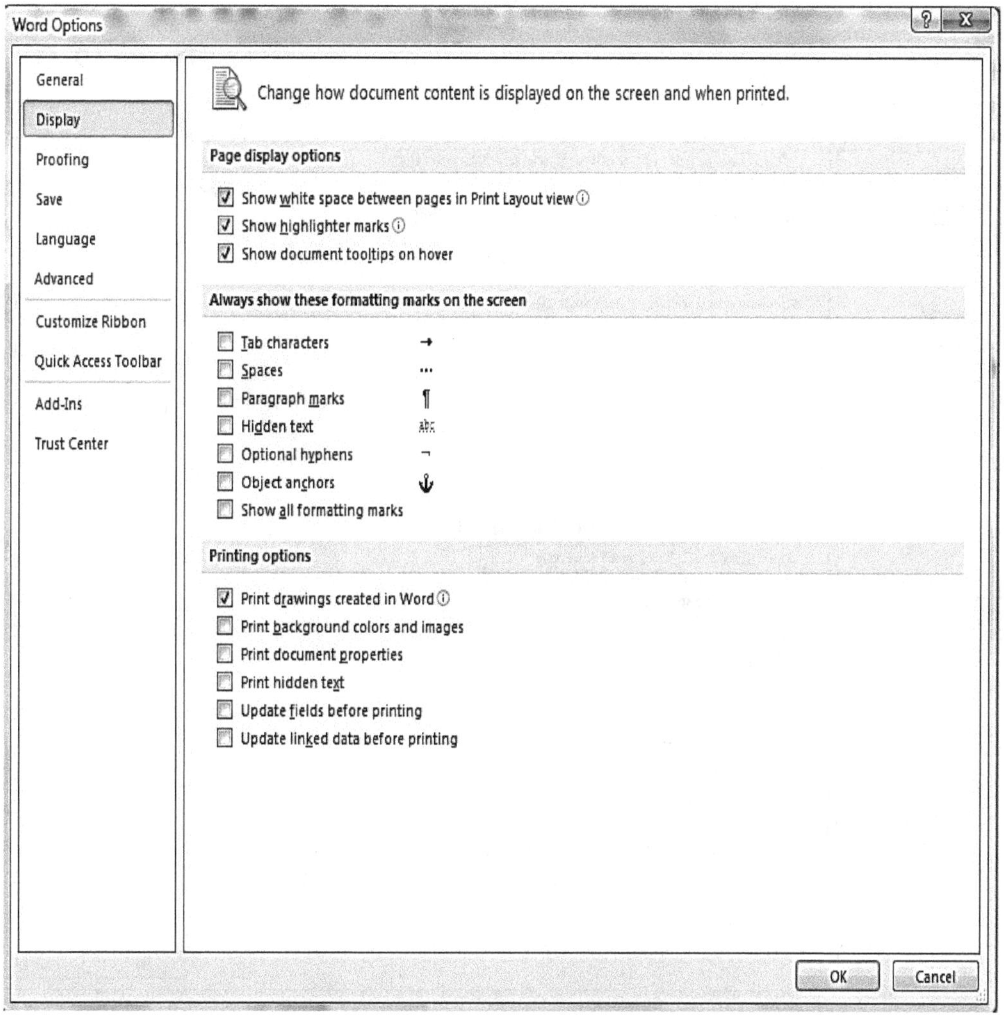

Proofing Options

Behind the Proofing Options, dialog box you can see and change how Word corrects and formats your text. Here are a few basics to consider. Notice that Word is set-up by default to ignore words that contain numbers, and to flag repeated words. The default options are indicated by the check mark (✓). You can turn off any of these options by clicking into the checkbox. Observe other settings such as Mark grammar errors as you type and Use contextual spelling.

In addition, the AutoCorrect database contains frequently misspelled and mistyped words, however you can add your own list of words by typing those words into the "Replace" and "With" fields.

Figure 18

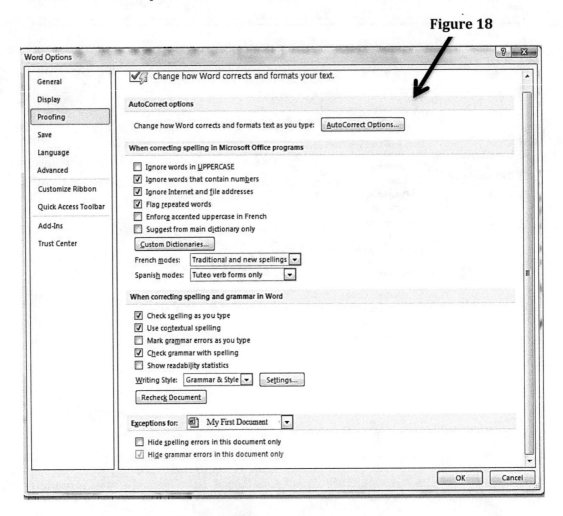

Again, as you become more skilled at using Microsoft Word, try experimenting with other AutoCorrect features.

Save & Back-up

To customize how Word saves and backs up your documents, you will need to explore the Save & Backup menu.   Here, you can adjust how often Word saves your file. Consider placing a check mark next to the Embed fonts in the file option if you are planning to share your files and want to preserve the fidelity of the fonts you have selected for your document.

Figure 19

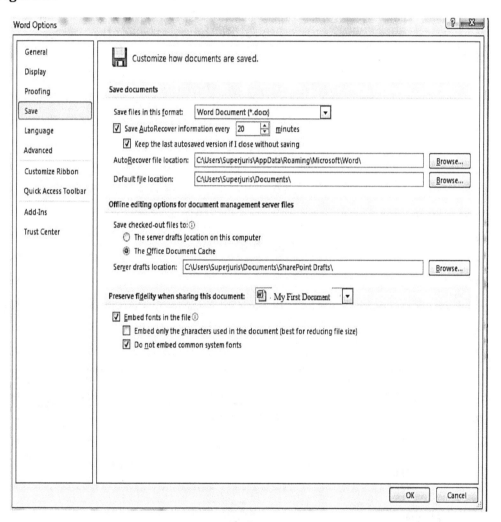

Mail Merge

If you want to send a single document to multiple people, you can save time with Word's mail merge feature. Word's built-in Wizard program will guide you through the entire process of combining a list of addressees with a letter. During this process, you are placing codes in your document that contain the information for each individual addressee. Once you have worked with merging letters, envelopes and labels will be easy to do as well.

I recommend that you create your list of addressees before you begin working with the merge feature. Using a Word table is a good way to create your list. In addition, we also recommend that you create the basic letter you want to send to the addressees first. Remember where you have stored your documents, as you will be required to locate them as part of the merge process.

Setting-Up a Mail Merge

1. Select the Mailings tab.

2. Click on the Start Mail Merge dropdown box.

3. Choose the Mail Merge Wizard option.

4. Select the document type or accept the default.

5. Click on the Next button and then follow the on-screen instructions.

Figure 20

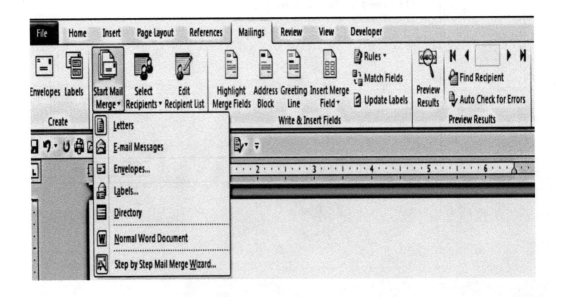

My Notes:

My Notes:

CHAPTER 4
WORKING WITH
VISUALS

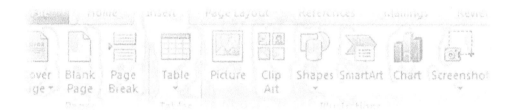

- *Create a Table*

- *Use the Table Styles Gallery*

- *Insert an Illustration into a Document*

- *Adjust or Size an Illustration*

- *Use SmartArt*

- *Place Shapes into your Document*

🕐 *The Estimated Time to Complete These Tasks is 11 Minutes*

Creating Tables in Microsoft Word

When you want to organize information, there is no better tool than a Microsoft Word table. A Word table can make it extremely easy to type and edit text. Fortunately, with a little forethought, you can put together a very polished and professional looking table. Moreover, Word comes with a gallery of styles for your table, and actually allows you to try them on before you apply them to your data.

See Figure 21, and observe how this table consists of three columns and three rows. In addition, the table also contains banded rows of alternate colors. Together these elements make up the Light Shading, Accent 5 Table Style. To create a table in Word you must select the Table dropdown box, located on the Insert tab.

To Create a Table

1. Select the Insert tab.

2. Click on the Tables dropdown box.

3. Click on the Insert Tables menu option.

4. Enter the desired number of rows and columns for your table.

5. Click on the OK button.

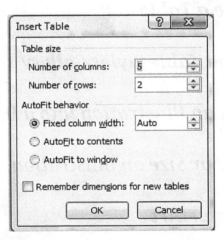

Figure 21

Column 1	Column 2	Column3

Make That Table Look Great!

The Design Ribbon

Enhance the way your table looks by using the Table Styles feature. When you double-click anywhere within your table the Design Ribbon appears. Simply click on the Design Ribbon, and then choose the desired table design from the Table Styles Gallery. See Figure 22. To try-on the various table styles hover with your mouse over each style option.

Figure 22

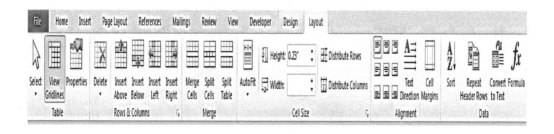

Course	Instructor	Location
Word	Martin	Berle Hall
Excel	Cunningham	Harris House
PowerPoint	Hampton	Berle Hall
Publisher	Guzman	Francis Hall

The Layout Ribbon

If you double-click within your table, Word also activates the Table Tools tab and the Layout ribbon becomes active. From this tab, you can choose to insert additional rows and columns. In addition, there is a Sort button, located in the Data Group. This feature is a wonderful and essential feature if you want to arrange data in ascending or descending order.

Placing a Picture into your Presentation

Pictures really do help tell your story, and fortunately, Word makes the placement of pictures and other media types within a document very easy to do. Clip Art contains a gallery of illustrations, videos, photographs and audio files that come bundled with Word.

In general, personal photographs are stored in your My Pictures folder. Therefore, if you want to insert the photograph you took of your dog Fido, choose the Picture button located on the Insert tab. On the other hand, if you are looking for some illustrations to spice up your PTA flyer you will want to open the Clip Art gallery. Place your cursor in your document where you want the picture, photograph, video or audio file to appear, and then perform the steps below.

1. Click on the Insert tab.

2. Select the Clip Art or Picture button.

3. Type the name of the object you want.

4. Click on the Go button.

5. Click on the desired image.

Adjust the Size of Your Photographs or Clip Art

After you select your photograph or clip art, Word places it into your document surrounded by handles. See the dog graphic in Figure 23.

To make the image larger or smaller, simply hover with your mouse over any of the handles, and notice the double arrow. When the double arrow appears, hold down your left mouse button to size the image. To delete a picture click on it, and when the handles appear, press the delete key on your keyboard.

Figure 23

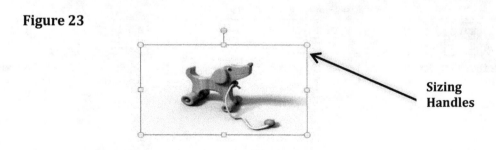

Sizing
Handles

Opened Clip Art Gallery

Figure 24

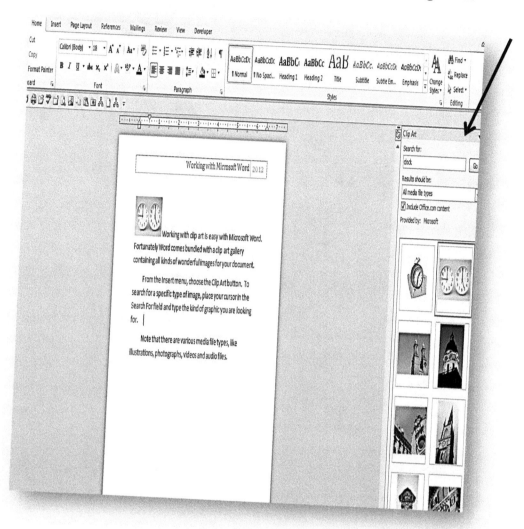

If you are looking for a particular type of graphic, type its name in the Search for field within the Clip Art dialog box.   See Figure 24.   For example, if you type the word **clock**, the Clip Art Gallery will display a number of clock or time-related images.

You can control the types of images the Clip Art Gallery retrieves.   For example, if you click on the Results should be field; you may choose to limit your search to specific media types, such as photographs, videos, illustrations and audio files.

My Notes:

Look Smarter With SmartArt

To create a visually appealing document, consider the use of Microsoft's SmartArt. The SmartArt gallery comes with more than 40 objects including organizational charts, flow charts and process symbols. See Figure 25 below. Creating an organizational chart is a common business practice. To become more acquainted with Word's SmartArt feature, try creating the organizational chart depicted below.

To Create an Organizational Chart

1. Select the Insert tab.

2. Place your cursor where you want the chart to appear.

3. Click on the SmartArt button.

4. Click on Hierarchy within the Navigation pane.

5. Choose the desired layout.

6. Click into the placeholders and enter the names and titles of the individuals.

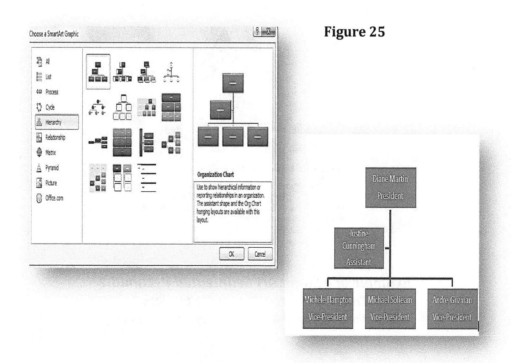

Figure 25

SmartArt Graphic Options *

<u>Lists</u>:   Select this option to create visual effects for bulleted items.

<u>Process</u>:   An option suitable for depicting routes, procedures and progression.

<u>Cycle</u>:   Represents a sequence of stages, tasks, or events in a circular flow.

<u>Hierarchy</u>:   Shows hierarchical information or reporting relationships

<u>Relationship</u>: Depicts connections, links, or a correlation.

<u>Matrix</u>:   Used for concepts, relationships sequenced or grouped blocks of information.

<u>Pyramid</u>:   Used to show containment, proportional, or interconnected relationships.

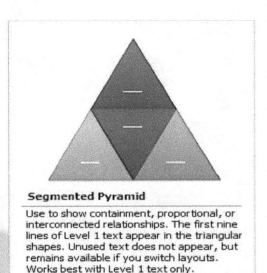

Example of a SmartArt Segmented Pyramid 1
Taken from the SmartArt Gallery
Descriptions adapted from the Microsoft SmartArt Galley

Working with Shapes

Word comes with a wonderful array of shapes you can use to enhance a document. Whether you need a rectangle, triangle, circle or star, Word likely has just what you need. You can find Shapes within the Illustrations Group, located on the Insert Ribbon.
See Figure 26.

To Insert a Shape

1. Place your cursor where you want the shape to appear.

2. Click on the Insert tab.

3. Click on the Shapes dropdown box.

4. Select the desired shape.

5. Hold down your left mouse button and then drag your mouse left or right to draw and size the shape.

Figure 26

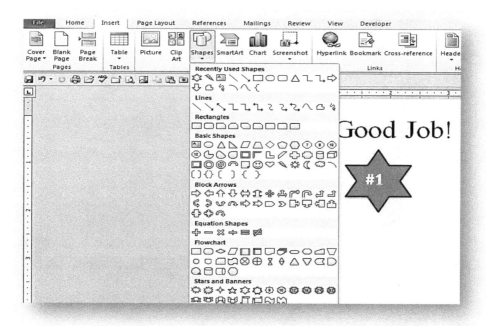

To delete a shape, click on it to select it. When the handles appear, press the delete key on your keyboard. You can use the textbox shape to place text over graphics.

Work with Templates

If you ever find yourself in need of a resume, fax cover sheet, book report or flyer, you will be pleased to learn that Microsoft Word comes bundled with a wonderful variety of pre-designed documents to kick-start start your project. You will also find these templates categorized by subject.

To Access Word Templates

1. Select the File tab.
2. Click on the New menu option.
3. Select the desired template.
4. Choose the Create button.

Figure 27

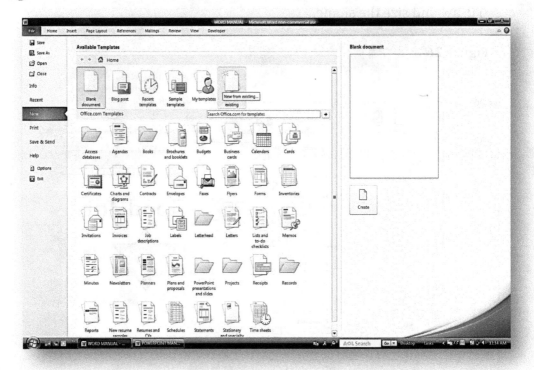

While many templates are installed on your hard-drive, additional templates may be downloaded from the Internet. If you do not see what you are looking for try the Microsoft website. There you will find an additional source of templates from both Microsoft and members of the Microsoft Office user community.

Word 2010 Templates Window with Fax "Clipboard design" template Selected

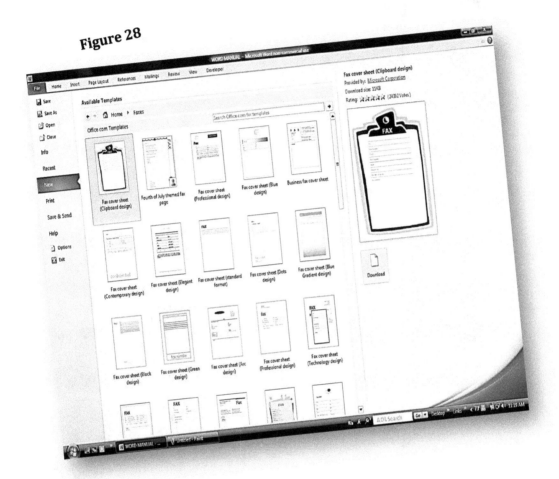

Figure 28

You can search for a specific template, i.e., resumes, flyers, invoices or statements by clicking into the Search Office for Templates field and typing the category name. See Figure 28 above. When you click on a template, Word displays a likeness of it for your review.

Do experiment with the different templates. In addition, do not be afraid to modify an interesting template in order to make it conform to your specific requirements.

An Example of Microsoft's Invitation Template

You're invited
to celebrate…

[NAME OF EVENT]
with us!

WHEN:

WHERE:

WHAT TO BRING:

DRIVING DIRECTIONS:

RSVP TO:

My Notes:

My Notes:

CHAPTER 5

MICROSOFT WORD RIBBONS & TABS

- *File Tab*

- *Home Tab*

- *Insert Tab*

- *Page Layout Tab*

- *References Tab*

- *Mailings Tab*

- *Review Tab*

- *View Tab*

- *Developer Tab*

The File Tab

Click on the File tab in Word 2010 and Microsoft displays what it calls the Backstage View. From this tab you can save files, access recently opened files, create a new document, print or exit the Word application.

Other Word features include the ability to place security restrictions on files, and remove personal information from your Word documents.

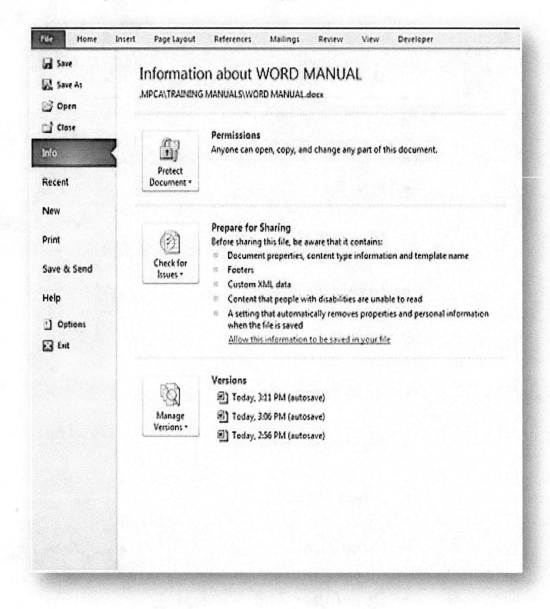

Home

The Home Tab displays a ribbon containing a host of text formatting options. Enhance documents by indenting, centering, justifying or right aligning text. Use and create styles to preserve formatted text for use in other documents or repetitively within the same document.

Insert

Click on the Insert tab to access features like Clip Art, Cover Page, WordArt, headers, footers and SmartArt to name a few. From this tab you can also draw shapes, create page breaks or insert a Microsoft Excel chart within your document.

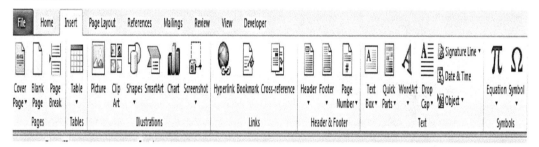

Page Layout

From this tab, you can apply colorful themes to your document, create multi-columned documents, change line spacing or place a watermark in your document. Here, you can use the Tracking dialog box to view and monitor changes to your document.

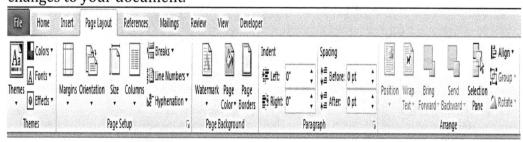

References

You will find the References tab handy for inserting footnotes, endnotes or citations into your document. This is also the site of the Table of Contents group functions.

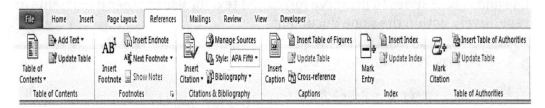

Mailings

Mail documents to multiple users easily with Word's Start Mail Merge group. To begin, type your document, and then select the Step-by-Step Mail Merge Wizard.

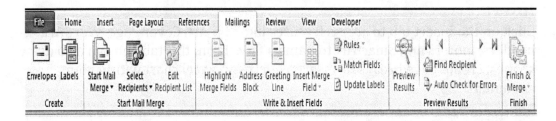

Review

Before you share a document with others, be sure you select the Review tab. You will find helpful features such as Spelling & Grammar, Thesaurus, and Word Count.

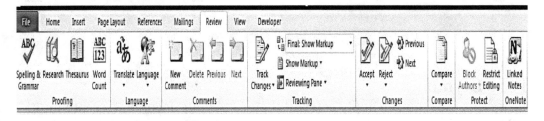

View

Use the Document Views, Show/Hide, Zoom and Window groups for various ways to examine and display your document.

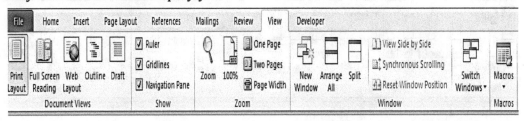

My Notes:

My Notes:

Online Resources

You will find a variety of helpful resources on the World Wide Web to assist you with Microsoft PowerPoint; below are just a few.

www.microsoft.com	➤ *Access templates, tutorials and the latest updates concerning Microsoft Office applications and products.*
www.certiport.com	➤ *Use this portal to obtain information on how to become a certified Microsoft Office Specialist.*
www.mypcassociate.com	➤ *Obtain quick reference cards for Excel, Word, Outlook and PowerPoint. Find out about how you can learn new Microsoft applications.*
www.pcworld.com	➤ *Keep up to date with the latest software and hardware products on the market.*
http://www.pcmag.com/	➤ *Check out PC Magazine's web site for the latest news, downloads, deals and product reviews.*
http://magazine-directory.com/Smart-Computing.htm	➤ *Smart Computing is another great web site if you want to keep abreast of what is going on in the land of computers.*

My Notes:

Appendix A --Practice Exercise

MS-Word

These exercises are designed to reinforce what you have learned about Clip Art, shapes, character formatting, bulleted text, footers, and using SmartArt to create an organization chart.

1. Create a flyer for the following event:
   Parmani Designs Sponsor of the Race for the Cure Corporate Marathon on Monday, January 7, 2013.

   a) The co-Sponsors are Tara Mang Fashions, Caramis Menswear, Trooks Brothers, and Bracy's Department Store. The Parmani motto is "Come and Make a Difference." The Race starts at the Central Park Arboretum at 2pm, rain or shine.

   b) Include a Clip Art image.

   c) Use an appropriate AutoShape.

   d) Create a centered heading using a 16 pt. bold font for the first line of the flyer: "Race for the Cure Corporate Marathon."

   e) List the co-sponsors using bulleted text.

   f) Create a footer and insert the following: Sponsored by Parmani Designs

   g) Save the document as Parmani Race.

2. Create an organizational chart for the following people:

   - Janice Wang, President.
   - Mary Morrison, assistant to Janice Wang.
   - Doug Jones, Vice-President.
   - Peter Roberts, Lynn Aniston, and David Pitt report to Doug, (All of them are Account Executives.)
   - Michele Parmani is also a Vice-President.
   - Nora Davis and Peter Mario are Account Executives. They report to Michele.
   - Include the Preparation date of this organizational chart.

Index

Quick access toolbar, 1-23

This Page Intentionally Left Blank

COMPUTE, EXCEL AND ADVANCE!

About the Author

Diane Martin is executive director of My PC Associate NYC. She has been teaching computer applications in the fields of business and higher education since 1981. In 1999, with a background in business and legal technology, Diane migrated to the field of higher education, becoming the director of computer networking and support for a college of business and technology in New York City. She subsequently taught Computer Applications for Business at the DeVry Institute of Technology, and the Laboratory Institute of Merchandising, both in New York City. She is currently on the faculty of Continuing Education at Long Island University. Diane is a member of the Association of Information Technology Professionals and the Association of Women in Computing.

In addition to a Juris Doctor degree, Diane also holds a Master of Science degree in Instructional Technology from New York Institute of Technology, and a Bachelor of Arts degree in Liberal Arts from Long Island University. She is a certified Senior Professional in Human Resources, (SPHR) a certified Microsoft Office Specialist, and she holds a New York State Business School Teacher license.

My Notes:

My Notes: